WARD,
HOPING YOU GET
ENOUGH "HUNTING"
IN YOUR LIFE.

THE HUNT

Photographic Locations Listed on Page 166

FLY FISHING'S
GREATEST ADVENTURES

THE
HUNT

by

SCOTT MUELRATH and DON MUELRATH

CONTENTS

23 ACKNOWLEDGEMENTS

25 FOREWORD

27 PHILOSOPHY OF THE HUNT

29 INTRODUCTION

30 TARPON

46 BROWN TROUT

62 BONEFISH

78 CUTTHROAT TROUT

92 SALTY PREDATORS

106 BROOK TROUT

120 PERMIT

134 RAINBOW TROUT

150 TROPICAL EVENINGS

162 ABOUT THE AUTHORS

164 GUIDES AND OUTFITTERS

166 PHOTOGRAPHIC LOCATIONS

Library of Congress Cataloging-in-Publication is available

ISBN 0-9769225-0-9

**To purchase *The Hunt*, contact the
authors, or to inquire about custom size
prints of the photos in the book,
visit the website:**

www.ffhunt.com

Printed in China by Regent - First U.S. Edition

Art Director and Producer:
Holli Scheumann, Innovative Marketing and Design
Design Consultant: Jeff Bright
Editorial Consultant: Michele Farver
Photography Consultants: Rick Lovie,
Steve Farrell, Oleg Kozyrevskiy

DEDICATION

There is one person whose name doesn't appear on the cover of the book or in the listings of acknowledgements or credits, but who has had a large role in the creation of The Hunt. She was the person behind the lens for many of the photographs in this book even though no credits are listed, because she specifically requested that her name not appear anywhere. She is the same person who used to worry during our early fly fishing days when we didn't arrive home until long after dark, wondering what could keep us out so late. She embodies many of the ideals that make fly fishing an attractive sport such as patience, kindness, a gentle spirit and a forgiving nature. She has enjoyed and endured many amazing experiences with us in the pursuit of our fly fishing passion, and has been there for the best and the worst. She is the heart and soul of the Muelrath family. She is Marte Muelrath, and with all the love we can muster, we dedicate The Hunt to her.

ACKNOWLEDGEMENTS

R. Valentine Atkinson and his photography have been an ongoing inspiration in our development as fly fishing photographers. Getting to know him personally has been a highlight of our fly fishing lives. We were honored to have him write the foreword for *The Hunt.*

Lani Waller put us on the path to fly fishing for the world's great gamefish over 20 years ago when he sold us Scott's first fly rod - a glass, Powell 7½ foot, multi-weight (5,6,7) rod. In Lani's "Philosophy of the Hunt" (page 27), he captures the essence and spirit of what it truly means to stalk a sighted fish.

On the "Guides and Outfitters" page, we've listed those who have played a role in our fly fishing excitement. Special recognition is given to Belize captains and guides, Martin McCord and Charles Westby, with whom we have been fishing since 1986. They can recall us arriving in Belize City with one bonefish fly rod, a rod case full of spinning rods, and a trunk filled with spinning reels and lures. Martin and Charles have been major contributors to our development as saltwater fly fishers.

Photographers who contributed images to *The Hunt*: R.Valentine Atkinson – 161; Dan Holden Bailey – 41; Terry Chick – 144, 145 (Bear charge); Josh Frazier – 33, 38, 39, 68, 71 (CI), 104 (RS); Brian Geis – 71 (LR); Tim Pask – 98 (GT); Rodrigo Sandoval – 58

Flys that apprear in *The Hunt* were tied by: Jim Arce – 65; Dave Ellis – 109, 112, 130 (crab); Pablo Negri – 130 (box); Clark Reid – 137, 141; Keith Westra – 153

Several other people have played varying roles in the *The Hunt*. Our thanks to: Tony Brookfield, Bob Cazort, Dan Ellis, Dave Ellis, Ed Farver, Josh Frazier, Bruce Goodman, Aaron Griffiths, Bob Haig, Damian Hedley, Wayne Henry, Jim Hine, Rich Hosley, Eddie Howells, Karl Kirbus, Laurel Kohl, Kim Laur, Buck Levy, Mark Makela, Betty McNairy, Jim McNairy, Jeff Mironuck, Richard Montgomery, Gary Neal, Bob Noyes, Trevor Prichett, Beau Purvis, Bob Rizzardi, Jody Scheumann, Gary Shontz, Jeff Slater, Jim Taylor, Michelle Tusan, Keith Westra, Julie Zion, Scott Zion.

FOREWORD

by R. Valentine Atkinson

I first met Don and Scott Muelrath in Mexico where I was working on a photo shoot for Casa Blanca, an Ascension Bay fishing lodge on the Yucatan peninsula. Don was carrying his camera bag around everywhere and he was constantly clicking away at anything that moved. He and Scott were down there to photograph as many species of fish as they could catch.

Every time I ran into him he had a question about photography for me. It seemed he had a thousand questions about film, f-stops, lenses and lighting. How do you shoot from boats, helicopters and airplanes? It was non-stop questions.

So here I was trying to do my job and the last thing I needed was someone following me around "picking my brain" about photography. It was starting to get on my nerves. I'll be darned if I didn't run into them again the very next year at the same place. It seemed like a plot. Only this year I noticed a difference. They had all the right photography gear and seemed to know a lot more about what they were doing (as it relates to fly fishing photography). And they were catching a lot of fish. I consistently saw them up each morning at dawn working their photography with the rich, beautiful morning light, and then they would return to the lodge each evening with exciting stories about big fish that they had stalked and caught – or not, but had captured the excitement of the chase on film. They were always energized, enthusiastic and very entertaining.

It was obvious that they had both learned much during the preceding year. Still it was a constant stream of questions at breakfast and dinner. They were a good team; father and son plying their newly acquired skills of photography and fly fishing on each other, learning by their mistakes and forging ahead into new territory. What they lacked in knowledge and know-how they made up for in enthusiasm and a great sense of humor, and I began to enjoy their company.

The fly fishing community is a rather small, intimate society of friends and acquaintances who aspire to fish in beautiful and exotic locations, and consequently we often run into each other; so when I next bumped into them in New Zealand I wasn't surprised at all. But this time I noticed they really had their act together and were answering some of my questions.

It turned out we all lived in the San Francisco Bay Area, so we made plans to get together for dinner. They invited me over to their home in Napa where I met the rest of the family: Don's wife, Marte and Holli, his daughter, a graphic designer who did most of the design and production for this book -- both very charming and lovely.

I noticed Don's studio was completely brimming over with all the latest and most up-to-date photography equipment and the walls displayed wonderful photographic prints taken from around the world on various fishing trips they had shared. It was then evident to me that Don had truly found one of his life's passionate callings in photography.

One of the exhilarating aspects of becoming published in the world of editorial photography is that there is always room for new talent. If one is willing to work hard, submit material and make new contacts and obviously has a modicum of creativity and technical knowledge, there's always "room for one more." Today's magazines, journals and newspapers have an insatiable appetite for interesting and entertaining articles and photographs.

Don and Scott have since gone on to become published in many of the best fly fishing publications in the country, and I give them a lot of credit to have come so far in such a short period of time. Now the whole Muelrath family has pitched in to produce a new and exciting book entitled *The Hunt*. This book portrays the thrill and excitement of the chase and the stalk, or "the hunt" with a fly rod as the "weapon." We've all heard the phrase "there's more to the world of fishing than catching fish." If shared friendship, love of the outdoors, solitude and craftsmanship are parts that make up the whole, then certainly the stalking and hunting of the quarry must be one of the top highlights. Regardless of the outcome, win or lose, it's the intense excitement of the hunt that is paramount and is captured in the stories and photos in this book. It's this spirit which provides us something to be savored and remembered for years to come.

So I invite you to sit back, relax and savor this fresh and innovative book, *The Hunt*.

PHILOSOPHY OF THE HUNT
by Lani Waller

My own fascination and analysis of the hunt began in 1953, inspired by the hard body, bright colors and delicate eye of my first trout – a seven-inch rainbow I pulled from the spring-fed waters of Northern California's East Walker River. At the time I knew little of the emotions I would now describe as an "amorphous gestalt" – a mysterious blend and collection of vague yet powerful desires and impulses, which apparently came from some unknown and distant source.

Many seasons later, editor and publisher John Randolph and I were on the phone yakking about the excitement of fishing, and all the "great anglers" we had encountered over the years and just what made them so damn good.

"The ones I've fished with," I said, "were not really fishermen at all. They were hunters."

Randolph replied: "You're right, Waller. I believe there are those among us who still have access to the perspective and the abilities we once had as aboriginals." He told me about a book by a man named Paul Shepard. "Get it," John said.

About six months ago I finally ran across a copy of Shepard's book, *Going Home To The Pleistocene*. According to Shepard, our essential human psychology was formed during the Pleistocene epoch, over several hundreds of thousands of years, as our simian ancestors ventured out into the plains and savannahs to hunt and stalk, to gather food and to avoid being eaten themselves.

Shepard argues that our ancestors did not see the world and nature as separate from themselves. Rather, they perceived it as a process of cause and effect, a process in which the hunter became an essential participant. They learned how to use that knowledge to succeed in the hunt. Shepard also believes this evolutionary process remains a part of our inherited genetic evolution and psychology – if you look for it.

So, let's flash forward 500,000 thousand years or more. Tyrannosaurus Rex has disappeared long ago; you're a little more erect now and your spear has been replaced by a five hundred dollar graphite rod, and a four hundred dollar reel. Some of the "old stuff" remains: the collection of flies you have in your vest, all carefully crafted from the skin, hair, fur and feathers of animals and birds, each designed to look something like the kind of food eaten by your prey, constructed to trigger the most primordial of impulses.

For the past twenty minutes you have been as quiet as you ever are anymore, observing, calculating, and pondering every movement without your cell phone or any thought at all except the image in front of you. There he is…just below the hanging sweep of a wet fern, a shadowy form rises silently, breaking through the surface with its immense back. It disappears into dark water. A few seconds pass. The form appears again, sips a natural insect from the surface, then descends once more in the column digesting its own prey and preparing for the next movement. Time stands still. No, that's not quite it…time has gone backward. A long way backwards.

The guide looks at you looking at the beast. It is a giant rainbow trout. The line uncoils in a rolling loop and the bogus bug, made from thread, a small sliver of steel, rabbit fur and pheasant feathers, drops perfectly in place. A ring appears in the water in coiling patterns of soft light. There he is; he sees it. You feel his weight in your fingers and wrist. You have him. He is yours.

Ladies and gentlemen of the jury, my position is this: After the sighting, the careful stalk, at the moment your arm came forward and your heart pushed against your larynx, and you delivered your offering to the unsuspecting trout – the feeding animal – you lost your ordinary self…if only for a moment. At that moment, you got what you came for, the whole enchilada, and at that moment you were no longer a civilized man or woman. You left all that far behind. That's the magic of fly fishing.

That's what this book so beautifully illustrates – the magic of the hunt, the pounding in the heart, and all the things we see and feel when you simply turn off the modern mind and get back to the guts of the matter.

INTRODUCTION
Why the Hunt?

by Don Muelrath, Co-Author

Puffs of dust kicked up with each step as the 12-year-old boy moved along the well-worn trail that encircled the lake. In one hand he carried a spinning rod and the other hand clutched a bottle of salmon eggs. He was walking deliberately, heading for a spot he knew was the "honey hole." This special spot was the place he anticipated the orange salmon eggs would tempt some of the thousands of rainbow trout that the Fish and Game Department's hatchery truck had released into the lake that week.

He hesitated as something caught his eye. Gentle ripples disturbed the water's glass-like finish near the bank, which was sheltered by the long boughs of a large redwood tree that extended some fifteen feet out over the surface.

Wanting a closer look, the boy set his rod down as he dropped to his knees and began crawling through the dry grass. As he quietly approached the shoreline, he saw the cause of the disturbance and froze. In the crystal clear water, a few feet from the bank's edge, a ten-inch rainbow trout was swimming in purposeful half-circles with his lips occasionally breaking the surface.

He appeared to be eating something, but what was not clear. There were several flies buzzing under the tree limb, and there appeared to be some insects wiggling on the water's surface. Entranced, the boy forgot about his "honey hole" as he lay there, eyes riveted on that rainbow.

That lake was one of several on Mount Tamalpais operated by the Marin County Water Company in Northern California. The boy's father took him fishing there two or three times a season. On their next few trips to the lake, the boy would rush to the spot under those overhanging branches in hopes of witnessing the same scene, only to be disappointed.

The boy was me, and it was that moment, lying under the redwood tree, when the passion to become a fly fisherman was born. Of course, I didn't realize it then, but there have been many times that I've reflected on that experience and the impact it had.

Today, fly fishers all over the globe are pursuing the opportunity to cast to sighted fish. Whether it's a twelve-inch brown trout in a small, spring creek or a 100-pound tarpon in three feet of gin-clear water on a saltwater flat, it's the excitement of the hunt that provides the fly fisher with the greatest thrills and most vivid memories. It's that attraction and the associated adrenaline rush that has created the boom in saltwater flats fishing in recent years.

Getting in the right position undetected.....making the perfect cast.....watching the fly move into the fish's window of vision....hoping it will be attractive enough that the fish will eat. It's in this scenario that the greatest challenges and thrills of fly fishing are found. Add that the finest fly fishing takes place in the most pristine environments on the planet, both freshwater and saltwater, and one can begin to appreciate the great attraction of sight fishing with a fly rod.

Does the fish need to eat the fly? Of course, watching the fish sip the fly, or in the case of a baitfish imitation, greedily attack it, does complete the episode of the stalk in the most satisfying manner. However, the spirit of the hunt stands alone with its own rewards, whether or not the fish cooperates and provides the final exclamation point. Some of the more memorable sight fishing experiences we've had did not result in an eat by the fish. The story of the stalk on page 123 in the permit chapter is a great example – the fish never ate, but that encounter is one the fly fisher will never forget (nor will I as the observer).

What we've attempted to do with *The Hunt* is to capture the challenge and the thrill of the stalk with a fly rod, both in text and on film. The stories related are some of our most exciting episodes with each species of fish – either experienced by us personally or by a partner with whom we were fishing.

In addition to the photos, each chapter has an introductory story about stalking the featured species followed by some interesting facts about that particular fish. To assemble the photos that make up *The Hunt*, it was our challenge to visit many of the world's finest fly fishing destinations and fish with some of the finest guides. That was our reward. Hope you enjoy.

THE
TARPON

This particular tarpon flat could provide the stimulus for saltwater fly fishing fantasies. Interspersed between the large expanses of pure white sand were starkly contrasting dark areas created by the turtle grass growing from the bottom. The turquoise-hued water over the sand complemented the brilliant blue sky that had been with us the entire day. In the distance, the waves of the Caribbean rolling over the Belizean barrier reef provided a picturesque accent. A light southeast wind gently rippled the sea as the tide pushed across the flat...

...With a gin-clear depth of about three feet, any fish moving over the sand would be visible from a considerable distance. A small jack could be easily spotted, while a large tarpon could look like a submarine. Conversely, the dark back of a fish swimming above the turtle grass was invisible, even within short casting distance...

The morning had been eventful. We'd had four decent shots at tarpon and two hook-ups. Both of the fish had been in the sixty-pound range. As is so often the case with the silver king, they provided some intense thrills for very short times as they cartwheeled across the surface before throwing the fly.

I was fishing with Charles Westby, a longtime friend and one of Belize' most respected guides. It was early afternoon and we were considering motoring to our mothership, anchored just a few minutes run from where we were fishing. Lunch, limeade and a break from the tropical sun seemed like a refreshing idea.

The skiff was quietly being poled across the water, about fifty feet from the edge of a turtle grass flat, when my lunchtime thoughts were spectacularly interrupted. Moving lazily off the dark grass bottom and onto the sand were two tarpon, a matched pair of seventy pounders. The fish were close and I immediately got my line in the air for the cast.

As I started to release the cast, I was stunned by the sight of a large shape about twenty feet to the left of the two fish I was stalking. It slowly wandered off the grass and onto the light bottom where its size was easy to comparatively calculate as its bulk dwarfed the others. Though the first two fish were within easy range, it was an obvious decision to quickly change targets.

As I began to redirect the cast, my only concern was to stay far enough left so that one of the first two fish wouldn't eat the fly and prevent a chance at what appeared to be a tarpon larger than any I had ever hooked. The cast and fly flew true, landing about four feet in front of the monster. A quick strip and the fish charged with a ferocity that was breath-taking. His forward motion carried his head out of the water.

The next thirty seconds were some of the most frantic of my fly fishing life. In the commotion, I wasn't sure what had happened. Was the aggressive charge at something other than my fly or had the fly been eaten? In a frenzied state, I began strip striking with my rod tip pointed directly at the fish and felt his weight resisting. The fish was momentarily surprised by the hook being literally pounded into his jaw by my repeated efforts and he lay there motionless...for a few seconds.

Then, amidst water exploding everywhere, he began a series of spectacular leaps. On some, he lifted his great weight entirely out of the water and crashed noisily to the surface, while on others, he would surge with the top half of his body visible. All in all, the tarpon covered about seventy yards with this acrobatic performance leaving Charles and me awestruck.

When he finally hit the water for good, line began peeling off my reel at an alarming rate as if the fish were determined to go to Cuba. Charles asked if I wanted to chase, and since I was in favor of doing anything possible to reduce the physical abuse that would be heaped upon my body from bringing this big boy to the boat, I yelled "yes."

Twenty minutes later, the slugging match was just taking shape. We could clearly see the fish about forty yards away so Charles shut the motor down. Occasionally, I could gain a little line, and then the tarpon would take it back, and sometimes more. To help pass the time as my arms began cramping from the strain, we discussed how big he was. Both of us agreed on at least 120 pounds with an outside shot at 140 depending on how deep the body was.

Then we made a fatal mistake — we began considering what sort of photos we would take with this rare opportunity. We were only into this frame of mind for a few seconds when the line went slack. In disappointed silence, we looked at each other for a moment and then began laughing. Planning fish photos before you had the fish in hand was usually a death-knell and both of us knew it.

After retrieving our line, we found that the twenty-pound class tippet section of the leader had separated. A fish like that tests every aspect of the tackle and there had been a weak spot.

What a fish and what an unbelievable performance he'd conducted! We were privileged to have shared the experience with him, even for that brief time. Our only regret was those photos we were planning...

A Silver King

Tarpon are arguably the greatest gamefish in the world. They are most prominently known for their spectacular, gravity-defying leaps, but tarpon also have the strength to make lightning runs several hundred yards into your backing. In addition, tarpon can grow to a very large size; the world record fly caught tarpon is 202 pounds...

...Perhaps most exhilarating is the fact that they often reside in very shallow water, providing an angler with sight-casting opportunities that can create an adrenaline rush unparalleled in any other fishing venue. Watching a big tarpon turn 90 degrees and then rise up to inhale a seemingly inconsequential fly offering in three feet of gin-clear water is a memory that will last a lifetime...

Their range can extend up the Atlantic coast to the northeast states and as far south as the lower reaches of Argentina, as well as across the Atlantic to the west coast of Africa. In all of these locations, tarpon have proven a versatile and adaptive fish, inhabiting bays, flats, estuaries and freshwater rivers. A unique feature which allows tarpon to live in diverse environments is its modified swim bladder. This allows the fish to gulp air from the surface, permitting it to live comfortably in oxygen-poor environments such as brackish, mangrove lagoons. When tarpon gulp air, they "roll" onto the water's surface, displaying their broad, silver sides and revealing their presence in environments where otherwise the angler would not be able to see them.

The tarpon is classified under the genus Megalops, which translates into "large-eyed." The conspicuous eye of the tarpon can be seemingly stared into when sighted on a clear, calm flat. Tarpon, also commonly called the "silver king," are layered with distinctively large, bright and silvery scales. When in the water, these fish have more of a greenish hue, often appearing quite dark along their backs. Several other defining characteristics of tarpon include a significantly elongated final ray on its dorsal fin. The maw is scoop shaped, and when opened to inhale prey it resembles a large bucket; the mouth can also prove very difficult in which to set a hook due to the bony plates lining the inside, especially along the upper jaw line.

In their larval and juvenile stages, tarpon survive on zooplankton and insects, eventually expanding their diet to include small fish and crustaceans. Mangrove systems provide a nutrient-rich environment where they are protected from larger predators by the sheltering web of roots. Baby tarpon (up to 30 pounds) are often found cruising amongst the roots of mangrove-lined shorelines and channels. They can prove frustrating targets in these environments and when hooked, launch themselves into the air, sometimes crashing down amongst the branches themselves. A young tarpon can prove to be the most acrobatic fish on the planet. As they mature, they become exclusively carnivores, feeding on large schools of mullet, sardines and many other baitfish.

The tarpon achieves sexual maturity around six years of age at a length typically of three to four feet. They are slow-growing fish; tarpon that grow in excess of 100 pounds are usually over 10 years of age, with the females growing larger and living longer than the males. Females can grow to over eight feet in length and live in excess of 50 years. A sexually mature female tarpon can produce an egg count of over 10 million eggs. The spawning migration of the tarpon in the spring and summer is a prime period in which to pursue them, especially in the coastal waters of Florida and many of the inshore flats of Central America. The adult fish migrate into the more shallow waters and flats of estuaries and bays where the larval hatchlings can quickly find shelter along the mangrove shorelines.

Having the opportunity to sight-cast to and hook one of these giants is considered by many the pinnacle of fly fishing.

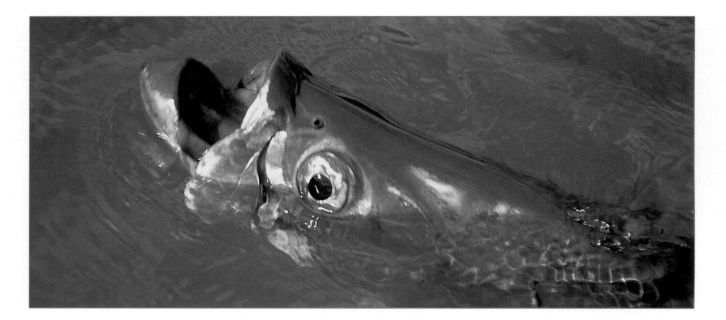

Tarpon Eats…

45 minutes later…

MOMENTS OF TRUTH...

Battles are decided at the gunnel of the skiff...

...and the edge of the mangroves.

Big fish…Big refusal

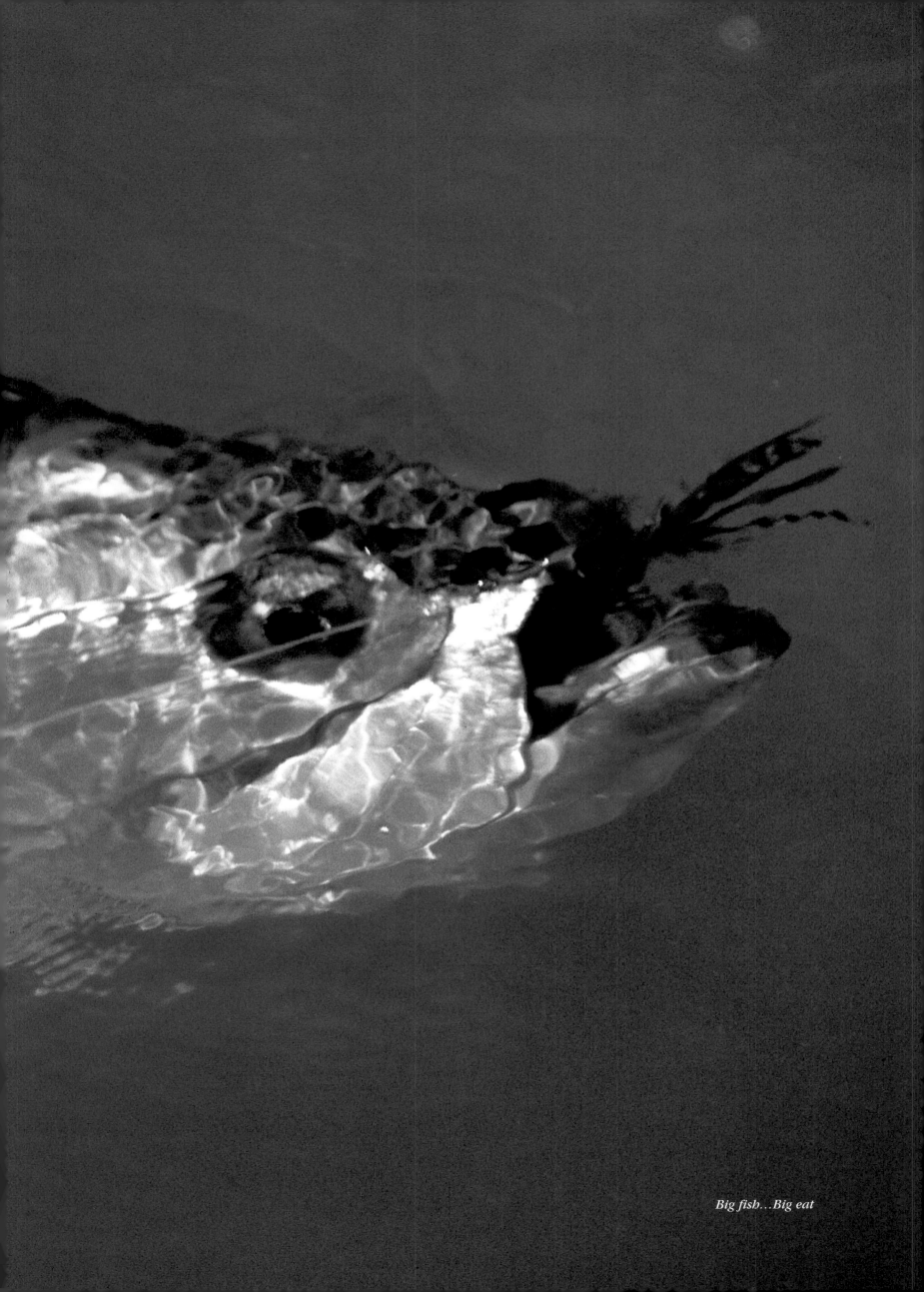

Big fish…Big eat

MANGROVES
The Tarpon Nursery

THE
BROWN
TROUT

It had been one of those magi-cal New Zealand days when the weather was perfect and big fish were cooperatively taking surface flies. It hadn't been a day of large numbers - we had only cast to seven fish all day, in addition to the half-dozen we stalked and spooked without making a cast...

...But the fish were spectacular, all of them in the five-to-seven pound range and one in double figures...

It was now late afternoon. Clouds were beginning to build and the sun had just fallen behind the snow-capped peaks of New Zealand's South Island Alps. Without direct sunlight, the spring creek on whose bank we were kneeling had lost its spectacular aqua color. The gunmetal gray surface of the water looked impenetrable, but that surface *was* being penetrated repeatedly by the nose of a trout sipping what appeared to be tiny caddis. Next to the huge nose of the fish, the flies appeared miniscule.

My companion and I watched the fish feed as we discussed fly choice and a strategy for approach and presentation. The only practical option was to position the caster downstream, behind the fish. Hopefully, the cast would deliver only the leader and fly above the fish to avoid spooking it by sight or sound of the fly line landing. For the fly, we selected the smallest caddis imitation we had – a #16 or #18. As aggressively as this fish was feeding, we thought anything near its eating window would get taken.

In New Zealand it is customary to take turns angling to spotted fish; this one was mine to hook or put down. Accordingly, I left the camera with my companion to record what would hopefully be an exciting episode.

I made my way downstream and quietly crossed the creek. Then, with as much stealth as possible, worked my way upstream until I was about 30 feet below the fish. I stripped off some line and began the cast. From my angle, I could see part of its back as it fed – it was a very good fish and I reveled in the chance before me.

The line was in the air and the cast looked like just the right length. The fly fell gently on the water...and immediately proceeded to rapidly "ski" downstream, creating a wake as it did.

Oops, a miscalculation! Our strategic planning hadn't taken into consideration all the factors at play. Upstream of the feeding fish the creek turned and split around a small island. The smaller, slower flow moved down the fork above the island, while the broader section flowed down the fork below the island and riffled directly in front of me. The fish held just below the island, facing into the smaller fork with its tail at the juncture of the two flows. The fly line had landed in the faster current just behind the fish, and while the fly had momentarily been in the right spot, the line immediately shot downstream, ripping the fly with it.

The fish was no longer feeding, nor was it visible. Had I blown a great opportunity? I looked back at my companion who returned my glance with a shrug of his shoulders. We waited a solid five minutes – it seemed more like an hour – and the fish reappeared, sipping as before. I had put him down, but thankfully he seemed recovered.

The only way I could keep the fly line from getting caught up in the faster moving water was not to allow any of it outside my rod tip. To get in position to do that, I would need to move precariously close to the fish. The only other option would be to wade upstream, get above the fish, and make a downstream presentation. In that case, I would get only one drift. If the fish didn't eat, it would certainly be spooked as the fly line was picked up from the water. I would have to get closer.

Taking a deep breath, I inched into the fast-moving water. As the current flowed around my boots it created a gurgling noise, which in my nervous state, sounded like Niagara Falls. The fish, however, did not seem to be disturbed. The sound of the merging riffles must have hidden my positioning.

Now barely over ten feet below, I could almost touch the tail of the fish with my rod tip. This should be easy – just fling the tiny caddis imitation above the fish and let the fly drift down to it. I waved my rod and repeatedly attempted to cast, but with a light breeze blowing down the canyon and without the weight of the fly line to assist, I couldn't get the fly above the fish. Again the trout dropped out of sight.

A few anxious minutes passed before it was back, rippling the surface. Frustration was setting in. I had become possessed with hooking this fish. We had developed a very special, one-sided relationship. We were so close I could practically count its spots. But this was not a cast I had ever made. I didn't know "dapping."

I had to get even closer. I cautiously took one small step and began again. On the fifth attempt, the fly finally landed a few inches above the fish's head. Up came the nose and the fly disappeared.

As my rod bowed to the resistance, there were two loud cries of excitement echoing across the valley floor. The large brown trout bolted upstream, then abruptly turned and charged downstream, just a few feet from my legs. Sometime later and a hundred yards down the creek from where the take had occurred, the fish tired and we took the final photos.

I had become a "dapper" with memories that will forever remain vivid. (*Photo essay on opposite page*)

A CHALLENGING QUARRY

The brown trout, known most commonly as the German Brown or the Loch Leven Brown (native to England), is generally recognized as one of the smartest game-fish in the salmonid family. This trout has both freshwater and anadromous populations native to much of Europe and parts of western Asia...

...Due to widespread popularity, the brown has been introduced to watersheds throughout the world. They were planted in North America beginning in the late 1800s, and subsequently in New Zealand, Australia, South America and Africa...

As with other members of the trout family, they have proven an adaptable fish that can develop self-sustaining populations, which thrive in both inland and ocean-fed environments.

Brown trout tend to grow bigger and live longer than their trout brethren. The fly-caught world record is 35 pounds, a sea-run fish from the Rio Grande in Argentina. They will resourcefully consume a variety of aquatic insects and invertebrates as well as other fish. While they can rise delicately and selectively to a well-presented dry fly, they are also known to attack crayfish, baitfish and mice imitations. Browns typically prefer structure, such as an undercut bank or downed tree. They rely on cover for both protection from predators and for ambushing unsuspecting prey. Brown trout are also frequently nocturnal feeders, making the larger, more intelligent specimens an even more challenging quarry. Because they are such a resourceful and aggressive trout, they are known to push out other fish from the prime feeding, holding and spawning waters. And as brown trout grow larger, other fish begin to comprise a significant portion of their diet. These traits have adversely impacted many native trout populations where browns have been introduced.

As its name would indicate, the brown trout is brownish in color, but there is a surprisingly wide variation in appearance. Generally, they are an olive-green to brown shade on the upper back, which often evolves to a golden-yellow along the sides and a gray or off-white color along the stomach. Spots on the brown trout are mostly black and usually more prominent and larger than on other trout. The spots are commonly bordered by a lightly shaded halo, adorning the mid-section and back, but rarely extending to the tail fin. Often there will be a row of red spots along the lateral line, although in the Loch Leven brown the red color is absent. Another distinguishing feature of the brown trout is the developed vomer bone located in the roof of the mouth. This bone is lined with "vomerine" teeth situated in a zigzag pattern. These teeth, which generally become more distinct as the fish matures, can prove sharp when the angler is trying to dislodge a hook set in the upper mouth.

Brown trout typically spawn during the late fall and early winter in a stream environment. During the mating season, the males develop a hooked lower mandible, similar to that of a salmon, and their yellow coloring becomes more vivid along the belly region. As with other trout, the female digs a redd with her tail, preferably in a gravel bottom. Up to two males will deposit sperm as the female simultaneously releases her eggs into the redd. Smaller brown trout under 12 inches can have an egg count in the hundreds; a large female over eight pounds might spawn over 6,000 eggs. The female will then move upstream of the redd and beat her tail fin on the bottom, sweeping gravel across the nest. The redd is then abandoned until the eggs hatch, which is triggered by warming water temperatures in the early spring.

As with other members of the trout family, brown trout have adapted to saltwater in certain geographies. Sea-run browns can grow quite large, such as those found on the very tip of South America at Tierra del Fuego. At this fishery, it is not uncommon to catch anadromous browns in excess of 15 pounds. But whether it is this prized sea-run specimen or a 10-inch brown in a tailwater, the brown trout is a challenging and highly sought gamefish.

THE MANY SHADES OF
BROWN

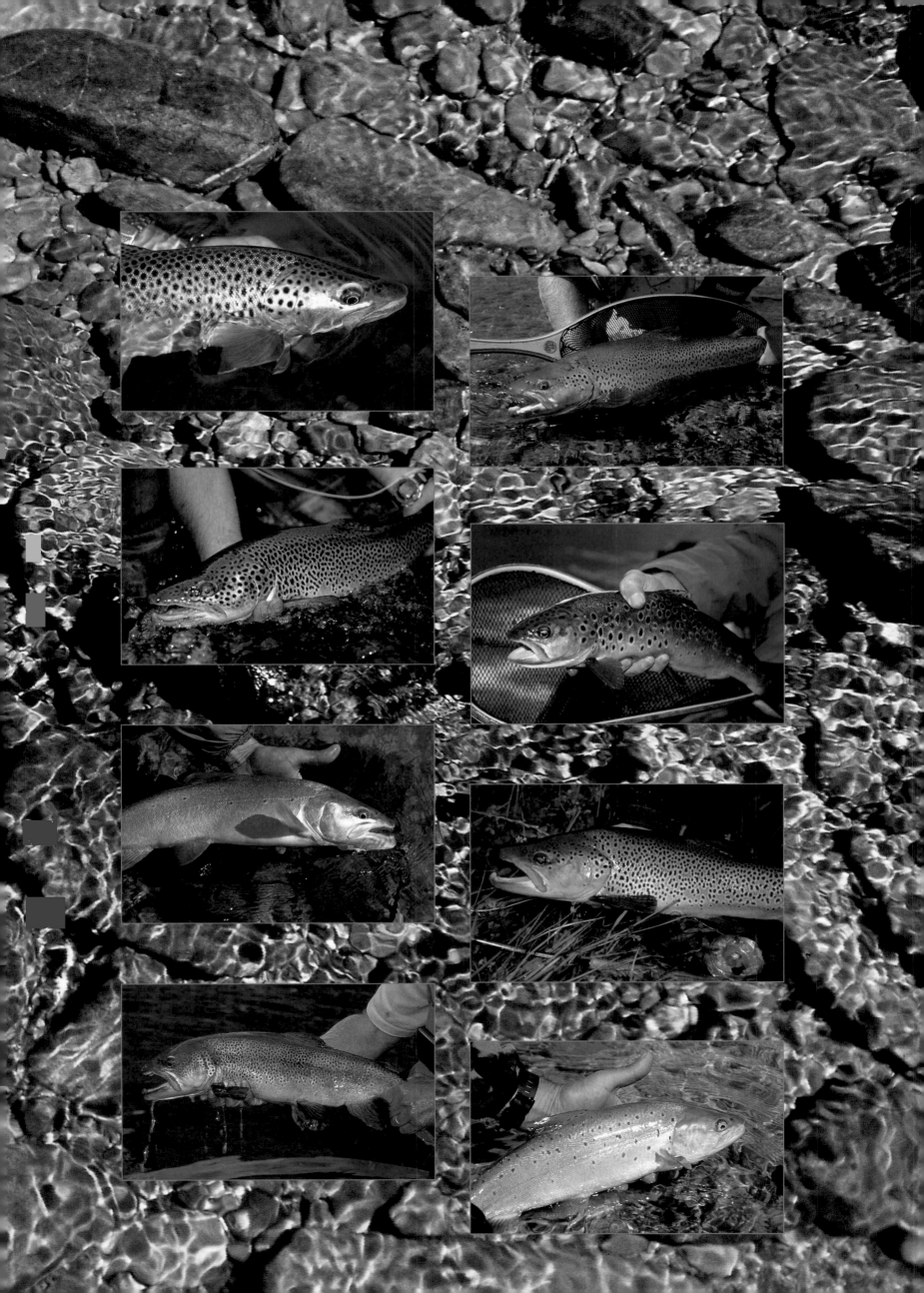

The sighting, the cast, the take, the battle…

...the chase, capture and release of a ten-pound plus New Zealand brown.

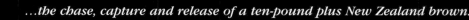

A Chilean stalking moon

Heaven via copter on the North Island, New Zealand.

Wintertime hunt on a Utah spring creek.

THE BONEFISH

"There."

I glanced over at the guide's outstretched arm, pointing off into seemingly oblivion. The vast expanse of the flats at Christmas Island stretched to the horizon, interrupted only by the occasional deepwater channel.

"Two o'clock, about 50 feet, swimming towards us, right on the edge…"

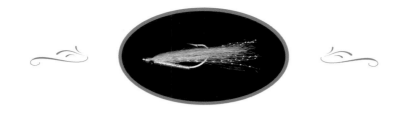

...I saw nothing. Although the guide had already detailed the location of the fish, my response was predictable.

"Where?"

"Right there. 40 feet. He's gonna see us."

His finger was pointing excitedly...

We had been stalking this particular bonefish for a few hundred feet. The fish was working along the edge of the flat, periodically moving off into the blue waters of the channel, only to return just when we thought we had seen the last of him. It was my first saltwater flats fly fishing adventure, and my rookie eyes were no doubt frustrating to the guide.

I saw the bone just before it was too late. I placed the cast about five feet in front of the cruising fish. The eyes of the Crazy Charlie pulled the fly towards the sandy bottom, about three feet down. One short strip and the fish propelled itself forward and inhaled its apparently easy meal. I set the hook and held on for the signature run.

The fish raced down the edge of the flat as my drag screeched. I never saw the fish clearly, although I knew it was bigger than average. It had been more a ghostly shadow due to the water depth where the flat faded into the channel. The fish spent the majority of the fight in the deeper water, occasionally moving briefly onto the flat, only to rapidly jettison back into the seemingly safer azure waters. After a few more blistering runs, which became shorter in duration, I could tell the fish had tired. Victory was imminent.

The line suddenly went slack.

"What happened?" asked the guide, as surprised as I that the fly would pull out at this late juncture. The flats in the area were void of coral or most anything that would sever a leader.

"Guess it popped out," as I began reeling up in disappointment. Certainly the stalk and the take, combined with the early scintillating runs, are the highlights of an encounter with a bonefish; but of course, every angler wants to finish full circle and release the prize. It was not meant to be this time.

The fish went well into my backing, so I was still reeling as my guide and I began looking over our shoulders back across the flat, wondering if maybe any bones were cruising up on us from behind. I glanced back out towards the deeper water when suddenly a fish bolted from the channel up onto the flat, swimming right for my feet. It happened so quickly I had no time to react as the bonefish smacked into my ankles and then kept swimming towards the center of the flat.

I yelped in surprise, as the reason for the fish's haste became immediately apparent. An ominous dark shape materialized a few scant feet behind the bonefish.

"Shark!" I yelled.

The dorsal fin of the shark sliced up and out of the water as its body pushed up onto the flat. It was maybe 4 feet long, but at that second in time it seemed more the size of a true man-eater. It was in hungry pursuit of my tired bonefish and swimming directly at me.

I instinctively jumped into the air. The shark brushed against my foot, no doubt as surprised as I. Its quest for a seemingly easy snack had been interrupted by the heel of my wading boot. The big fish turned tail and swam back into the channel before my feet hit bottom.

At that point, my fly rod nearly lurched from my hands. The bonefish had not shaken the fly after all, but had detoured directly back towards me with the predator in pursuit, seeking the sanctuary of the shallow flat. My angler instincts kicked in as I immediately raised the rod and once again began playing the fish for a second time.

It did not take but a few minutes before we landed the exhausted bonefish. It proved to be a large specimen, probably the biggest bonefish I have caught to date. With a bemused smile, the guide released the prize.

BUILT FOR SPEED

Newcomers to saltwater fly fishing most often select the bonefish as their first quarry. The reasons start with availability; there are far more plac-  *es where bonefish are readily found than other saltwater trophy species. The rods, reels, and lines used closely resemble stout trout fly fishing equipment, making the transition from fresh to saltwater inexpensive and familiar. And, bonefish are plentiful so the action tends to be faster than pursuing tarpon or permit…*

…The bonefish provides a memorable first impression and target. The excitement of hunting and sight-casting on shallow saltwater flats becomes readily apparent as an angler learns how to spot fish in the "skinny water"…

The speed and power of the fish, given its relatively small size, provides a genuine thrill. Even a two- or three-pound bonefish can penetrate deep into the backing on its first run.

Bonefish are primarily a coastal species which inhabits warm, temperate waters. While they may be found in North America as far north as New York in the east and San Francisco in the west, it's the tropical climates where they are pursued. The most popular destinations where they are sought include the Bahamas (where bonefishing with a fly was first developed), Florida Keys, Seychelles, Los Roques, South Pacific and in many waters throughout the Caribbean.

Bonefish prefer intertidal flats and mangrove-lined shores, and usually do not stray too far from deeper cover such as a channel. They can be found on sand, grass and coral flats, and amongst the mangroves. On an incoming tide, bonefish swim onto the flats to feed. They may be found in large schools of over 100 fish, or often as individuals, especially when the specimen is a larger fish. As the tide falls, the fish will usually leave the flats for the protection of deeper water.

Bonefish are notoriously skittish when foraging for food on the flats. The mere shadow of a fly line crossing over a single fish can often cause the whole school to panic, sending the fish back into an adjoining channel and the angler off to look for another flat. Ideally the angler will find the fish tailing, which occurs when the bonefish uses its conical snout to rummage through the grass or sand in search of prey, such as crabs, shrimp, worms and fish. When its nose is down, the tailfin emerges from the water as the fish tries to leverage itself while foraging. When tailing, bonefish are most easily approached as they are preoccupied with eating. The angler can often delicately place a fly within inches of the fish and have a decent possibility of a hook-up. If a bonefish is not tailing, they can be remarkably difficult to see, as their bluish-green back blends in easily with the surrounding environment. Because of this ability, they are commonly known by such names as the "gray ghost" or the "ghost of the flats." If water is more than a few feet deep, they are virtually impossible to see, and the angler must look for a "mud" created by feeding bonefish stirring the bottom.

The body of a bonefish is built for life on the flats. The mouth is full of granular teeth, which cover the tongue and upper jaw, and they have grinders in the throat, which make for easy processing of shellfish and crustaceans. Their blue-green backs enable them to blend in with their surroundings, even in water only inches deep. The body is sleek, round, compressed and built for speed, whether it is trying to break free from a hook-up or evading a barracuda.

A bonefish attains sexual maturity at the age of two. They can spawn year-round, although the primary months are recognized as November through June. Spawning usually occurs in deeper water, not on the flats. During the larval stage, bonefish are actually shaped like an eel and most of the fins are absent. The fish then goes through a metamorphosis, and the entire body shrinks to roughly half its initial size. Eventually the fins and scales develop, and once it attains a few centimeters in length it enters the fry stage. Juvenile bonefish have a series of dark bands that cross the back and run to the lateral line. As the fish matures, these bands eventually fade and are replaced by longitudinal streaks of a similar dark shade. Bonefish can achieve weights in the double-digit range, with the current fly-caught world record being over 15 pounds.

CLASSIC BONEFISH FLATS

South Pacific

Andros Island

Christmas Island

Belize

Los Roques

Ascension Bay

Northern Edge of Espiritu Santo Bay, The Mexican Yucatan

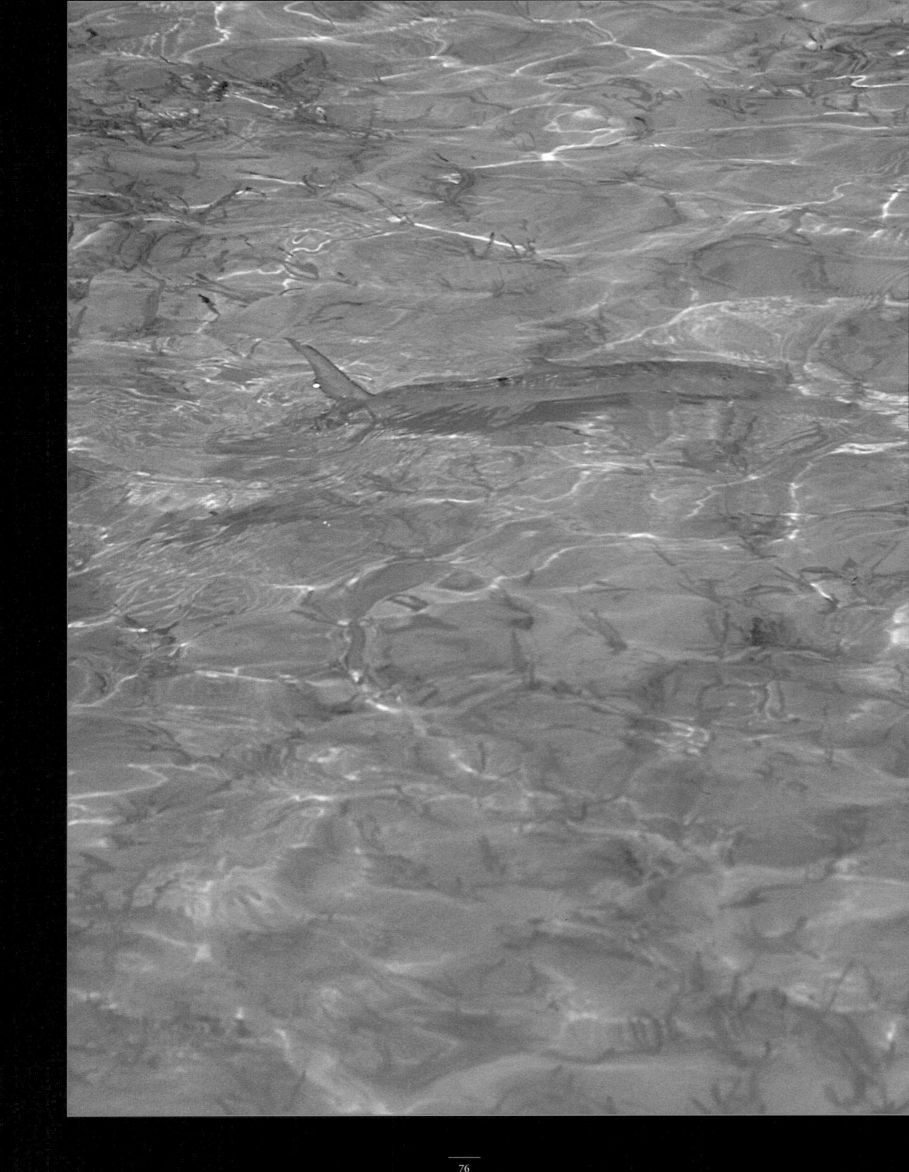

Roseatte Spoonbills surveying the flats.

THE
CUTTHROAT
TROUT

We were on our hands and knees about 100 yards upstream from where

the crystalline spring creek emptied into Wyoming's Snake River. Forty feet

upstream and a few feet off the far bank, the glassy surface of the water was

being constantly disturbed by a single working fish. Since we couldn't see

any insect activity on the surface, we guessed that the fish had positioned

himself to feed on a hatch of midges. It was feeding, rippling the water every

10 or 15 seconds as it gently sipped from the surface.

Cutthroat Country: *The Teton range is part of the border between Wyoming and Idaho. The Teton River in Idaho (top photo) and the Snake River in Wyoming (bottom photos) are home to the native Yellowstone and Fine-Spotted Snake River strains of cutthroat.*

…Even though the sun had dropped behind the majestic, snow-capped Tetons, we could see enough of this fish to realize it was in the 18-20 inch range. Most likely, it would be the largest fish we would cast to all day – if we could actually get a cast off before our presence was known…

Like spring creeks everywhere, this "skinny water" created an environment that caused these native fine-spotted cutthroats to be extremely wary. We had spooked several feeding fish already, without even making a cast, as we'd worked our way up this creek from where our guide, Tom Rowland, had beached his drift boat.

Tom whispered that finding a fish so large in this small spring creek was very unusual. Most likely he'd wandered up from the main river for a temporary feeding foray.

The decision confronting us was whether we attempt to improve our position so we wouldn't have to make a presentation from the disadvantaged angle currently presented to us. We decided not to risk moving even one more step. At the least, we wanted to find out if this fish would take our fly before we sent it scurrying for cover.

It was mesmerizing watching him glide in the flow of the stream. We were sharing one of nature's special moments as we observed this finned creature instinctively doing what he had learned from the past generations

of his kind. What grace a surface-sipping trout displays!

My trance was broken by Tom's softly spoken question, "Well, do you want to give it a try?" I replied with a smile and a nod.

The first two casts were too far to the right of the fish and our size 18 Griffith's Gnat floated by without getting his attention. Most importantly however, we hadn't disturbed the fish. It was still feeding, unaware of our intrusion.

The third cast placed the fly about five feet above the fish and just a little to the right of its feeding window. From where we were kneeling, this was as close as we were going to get without the presence of the fly line ending our pursuit.

The fly began its drift and we held our collective breath, hoping it would be close enough. We were lucky. The fish moved to the right, and in the unique style of a cutthroat, rose ever so deliberately and sucked in the imitation without the slightest hesitation. The hook was set and the cutthroat bolted upstream in a frantic state.

After some nervous moments when the fish entangled himself in vegetation and threatened to part the 6X tippet, the net slipped under him.

The red/orange slash under its jaw classified the fish as a cutthroat. This general area is home to both the native Yellowstone Cutthroat and the Snake River Fine-Spotted Cutthroat. The pepper-sized spots (as opposed to the larger spots that identify a Yellowstone Cutt) confirmed this one was of the fine-spotted variety.

A few moments to revive him and he was returned to the same environment that has been home to his species for centuries.

THE SLOW RISER

The first time you net a cutthroat will reveal the obvious reason for its name; this fish displays a very distinctive reddish-orange "cut" visible outside and below the lower jaw. There are numerous sub-species, including the Lahontan, Piute, Rio Grande and Westslope. The cutthroat can be found in both salt and freshwater, ranging in habitat from Prince William Sound, Alaska to

the Eel River in northern California, and inland throughout the western United States and Canada...

...The freshwater cutt has historically not competed well with other gamefish due to its tendency to hybridize, especially with rainbow trout, as well as experiencing over-harvesting by fishermen. While this has depleted many wild and native populations, the cutthroat has proven resilient in regulated waters...

When compared to its trout brethren, the cutthroat does not take to the air as a rainbow or provide a tug-of-war as with a stubborn brown, but they are still recognized as a premier gamefish. They employ other tactics, such as twisting and turning their bodies 360 degrees attempting to dislodge the hook. Inland cutts rise readily to a dry fly. Often they materialize lazily under your imitation, following it down-river just under the surface before they decide to either grab it on a down-river take or opt to slowly drop back into the depths, denying you the rise.

Depending on the geographic region, cutthroat display a broad range of coloring schemes. Inland fish have body colors including cadmium to a yellowish-green, and some strains develop red tinges on the head and body as well. Spotting can range from large and dark but few in number, to a more heavily but fine black-spotted pattern, such as found on cutts in the Snake River. When cutthroats interbreed, their native colorings often become the less-dominant pattern. The common cutthroat-rainbow cross, known as the cutt-bow, appears as a rainbow, with the genetic mix sometimes only revealed by the signature orange or red cut around the jaw line. The sea-run variety will have more of a silvery sheen and frequently display greenish-blue bodies with numerous heavy, black spots.

All subspecies of cutthroat possess the familiar redd-forming behavior pattern of the salmonid family, typically spawning in late winter or spring. Coastal cutts typically migrate to an estuary or ocean environment within their first three years of existence, usually returning to freshwater after approximately one year in the salt. Anadromous cutts usually spawn during the first winter or spring while in freshwater; however, at times they will make a second saltwater migration before spawning. They can spawn repeatedly. Sea-run fish can live past 10 years of age, and while they can attain double-digit weight, four to six pounds is considered large. Inland cutthroat live approximately 6 to 8 years of age and seldom exceed weights of 6 pounds (excluding the Lahontan strain), the world record hitting the scales at 14 pounds, one ounce.

The history of the Lahontan strain of cutthroat trout is especially unique. In its native habitat, this inland giant achieved weights in excess of 40 pounds. It inhabited the Lahontan drainage, which encompassed waters in western Nevada, the eastern slope of California's Sierra Nevada mountain range and southeast Oregon. This subspecies has a unique quality of being able to thrive in high-alkaline, desert lake conditions, waters in which other trout struggle to survive. During the early 1900s the Lahontan cutthroat was so plentiful that they were fished commercially, primarily being sold in the San Francisco Bay Area at prices of over $0.50 a pound. However, habitat degradation, both man and drought induced, as well as over-harvesting led to a rapid decline in fish counts. Its original habitat range has significantly dwindled, but thanks to research and resulting management plans, the Lahontan has survived in some of its native waters, such as Pyramid Lake, Nevada.

Cutt-bow: *cutthroats and rainbows often crossbreed with each other creating a hybrid, the cutt-bow.*

BRITISH COLUMBIA COASTAL RANGE CUTTS

A stealthy approach is needed for the Yellowstone Cutthroats in this Idaho spring creek near the headwaters of the Teton River.

On a Wyoming spring creek, an angler stalks a Fine-Spotted Snake River Cutthroat.

THE SALTY PREDATORS

It was late afternoon. We had

returned to the lodge following

a productive day of bonefish-

ing in the northern flats of

Ascension Bay, but I still wasn't

quite ready to set the rod down

until the morning…

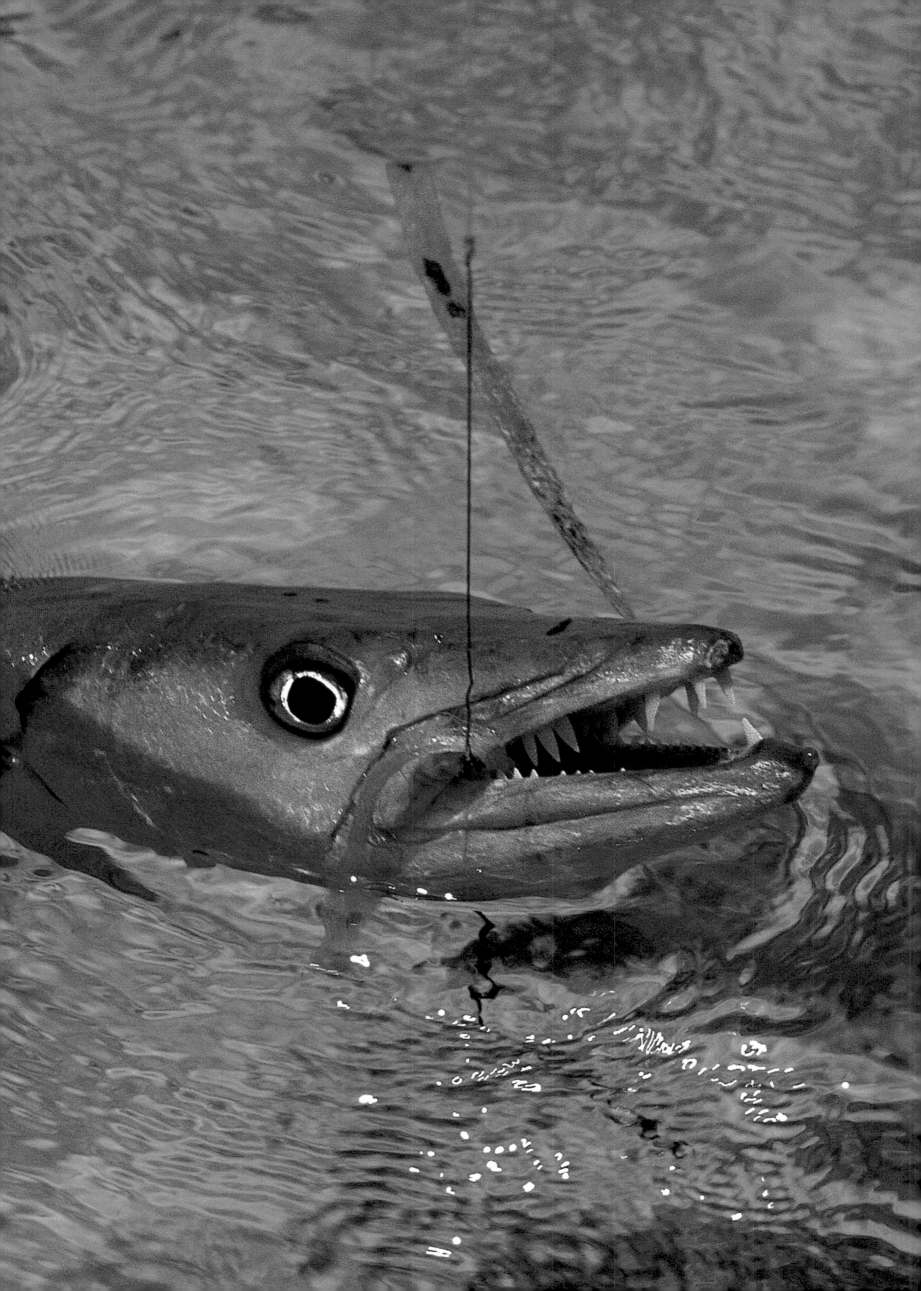

...Our guide had talked of sometimes being able to walk the beach and sight-cast to big snook, tarpon and other gamefish feeding in the surf. That was enough incentive for us...

After returning most of our gear to the room, my wife Michelle and I were on our way to the surf zone with an eleven weight in hand.

It was a beautiful afternoon as we walked the shore. The sandy beach sloped up on our right, abruptly ending at the jungle's edge. To our left was the broad expanse of the Caribbean, the water merging with the blue sky way out on the horizon. Waves gently rolled onto the beach, their ferocity greatly tempered by the long barrier reef which ran parallel to the coastline about 300 yards out. The white sand bottom extended about 20 yards into the sea, at which point it darkened due to grass growth and the presence of coral. It would be easy to see any fish of significant size if it were above the sand, although it was only about four feet deep where the bottom darkened. I doubted that we would encounter any big, predatory fish that close to shore under the glaring sun. My doubts were abruptly proven wrong. About a hundred feet up the shore from us was an easily visible pair of big jack crevalles. The fish were so far up in the surf zone that their golden backs were exposed as the waves retreated back to the sea. It was a bit puzzling to me why the fish had seemingly placed themselves on the threshold of being beached. They were moving leisurely, swimming in the same direction we were walking, but slowly enough that our pedestrian pace had caught up with them.

I observed a few more seconds. The pair made no sudden movements; the frenetic pace at which most jacks usually swim was completely absent. Unhurried, they proceeded down the shore, side by side, their broad backs and fins exposed with every receding wave. It seemed the equivalent of a romantic stroll, although I strongly suspected they were feeding on something they found to their liking in the churning waters.

Regardless, what I needed to do was obvious. With the fish swimming away from us, I wanted to place myself in front of them for the cast. Otherwise I risked lining the fish. With a few words of encouragement from Michelle, I circled up high to the edge of the sand and ran a couple hundred feet alongside the jungle's edge, keeping an eye at all times on the jacks. When I thought I was far enough ahead of the fish, I dropped back down to the water and waded into the breakers, relying on the noise of the crashing waves to hide my presence. The pair never altered course or changed pace. They were coming right at me. I just had to keep my composure.

It was going to be a short cast, as I did not want to lose control of any excess line in the breakers. I needed to place the fly, a blue and white weighted Lefty's Deceiver, in front of the fish and time its landing between waves to allow them an opportunity to see its movement. Thankfully, the wind was nothing more than a light breeze.

At fifty feet I began to cast. One false and then I let it go. The jacks were impressive specimens, especially in such shallow water. I was close enough to see their mouths open and close, grinding away at some morsel they had inhaled in the roiled surf. The cast landed too far to the left of the lead fish. It wasn't going to see it. I simultaneously back-pedaled and picked up the line, casting again. The noise of the waves covered my faulty effort and churning legs. The second cast landed true, about a foot directly in front of them. The fish were only about thirty feet from me as I gave the fly a hard strip. In unison, the two fish surged forward as they competed for the easy meal. I could practically look into their eyes as the lead fish engulfed the fly twenty feet from me.

I reared back and slammed the hook home. Not many fish can generate the powerful run a big jack makes upon feeling the hook. It was a reef-bound freight train as my drag screeched furiously in resistance. The fish was halfway into my backing before it finally slowed and the slug-fest commenced. It took about 30 minutes to subdue the jack, at which point I tailed it in the surf and removed the fly.

This particular fish was as golden hued as any I had ever seen. Truly spectacular, and a stalking experience I would never forget. (*Photo essay on opposite page*)

This baby grouper beat a bonefish to the Crazy Charlie.

SERIOUS TEETH

Needlefish

Lemon Shark

Black Tip Shark

Saltwater Crocodile

Barracuda

SHALLOW WATER VARIETY

The variety of saltwater fish that can be taken in shallow water with a fly and a floating line is extensive. Some of the more common species include the following:

Portuguese Man-of-war

Snook – found generally in or near the shelter of the mangrove roots, but sometimes located in open water or near rocky structure. This stealthy predator provides challenging target casting opportunities, occasionally to fish sighted on the edge of the mangroves, but more often, you are spot casting to pockets in the roots.

Jacks – aggressive feeders that are found in both small and large schools. Jacks can attain large size; fish of 20 and 30 pounds are not unusual. Strong fighters with an assertive nature, they will attack almost any fly, even if the presentation is not perfect. The most common Atlantic and Caribbean species are the Jack Crevalle and the Horse-eye Jack. The Pacific members of the Jack family include the trevallys: golden, striped, giant and blue.

Snappers – over 10 varieties, including cubera, dog, grey, lane, mangrove, mutton, red, schoolmaster, silk and yellowtail. Tough, structure oriented fish, they are found near the mangroves, reefs and rocky edges.

Barracuda - because of his size, speed, aggressiveness, and aerial antics (fish over five feet long can be found on shallow flats), the 'cuda is an electric "skinny water" fly rod fish.

Sharks – some varieties of sharks, such as the black tip and lemon, frequent the flats and will eat a fly. They are fun to watch approach a fly or popper as their eyesight is very poor; the fly almost has to be placed in their mouth.

Dorado, sierra mackerel, skip jack tuna and rooster fish can be sight-cast to along Pacific coastlines and bays.

Giant Trevally

Golden Trevally

Blue Fin Trevally

The atolls and reefs of the South Pacific are home to the Trevally family.

The Pacific Coastline of Central America offers sightcasting
opportunites for rooster fish, dorado and skip jack tuna.

Sightcasting along the mangrove roots for snook.

The Snapper Family

Mangrove Snapper

Cubera Snapper

Red Snapper

Schoolmaster Snapper

Mutton Snapper

Dogtooth Snapper

Grey Snapper

Yellowtail Snapper

Snook

THE
BROOK
TROUT

The fish we were stalking broke the placid surface and sipped a freshly emerged mayfly. It was a classic head-to-tail rise, displaying a broad, dark back. Even from our vantage point 100 feet away, we could tell this was the sort of fish that warranted the distance we'd traveled to find him...

...Again, about 10 feet to the right of his first rise, another brown drake disappeared and heavy ripples disturbed the late afternoon waters...

Our guide, Ray Best, with a praticed stroke of his paddle, quietly inched our canoe closer to the cruising brookie with the hope that he would continue to show himself. There were countless drakes covering the water to sustain his desire to satisfy the hunger left over from a long, cold, Labrador winter. The scene was vintage. Sitting low in the sky, the evening sun was emitting golden rays creating a warm glow on the black spruce covered slopes that descended around us to the edge of the Minipi River.

This image was burned into my memory banks decades ago while watching the popular outdoor television series, *The American Sportsman*. The series host, Curt Gowdy, and the legendary fly fisherman/explorer, Lee Wulff, filmed their visits to this fabled brook trout fishery. Watching those big brookies on my television screen as they gulped dry flys made an unforgettable impression.

My son, Scott, readied himself in the front of the canoe as we closed to within casting distance. Once more

the giant brookie nosed the surface, again to the right of the last eat. He seemed to be moving consistently to the right in his feeding ritual. Scott quietly dropped his cast on the water about eight feet from the last rise on the imaginary line the fish seemed to be following.

Predictably, the fish rose and engulfed the imitation. The line came tight and the rod tip dipped toward the water. The reel screeched as line peeled off the spool and the finned trophy offered the expected resistance.

After several tense minutes of give-and-take, the fish was near the boat; Ray gently slid the net under him. We attached the scale to the net above the fish, which verified our reason for excitement; the scale registered just over seven pounds. He was brilliantly adorned with the spectacular colors of a male in full spawning dress. His lower third was magenta red. The spots near the lateral line were splashes of blue, yellow, and red. With his lower body fins rimmed in pure white, the contrast between the dark, rich red in the rest of the fin made these appendages artful pieces of nature's work. A brookie carrying these colors is arguably the most beautiful of all freshwater fish.

The hook was removed, the fish gently revived, and Ray, a 25-year veteran of guiding and preserving this special fishery, released him.

The Perfect Model. *After grabbing a skittering mouse pattern in a tailout, this 6.5-pound male brookie was a photographer's dream. He lay motionless across the net for a full two minutes with his head just under the surface, pumping water through his gills. Following his short modeling career, he was released with care.*

A COLD WATER CHAMPION

Brook trout are a native species to North America. Their original habitat was limited to eastern Canada and the northeastern waters of the United States, but because of aggressive planting, they currently can be found around the globe. A common story applies: the encroachment of man and overharvesting have impacted native populations and reduced the original, natural realm of this beautiful game fish…

...In the United States, brook trout are often stunted in growth due to less than ideal habitat including overcrowded fish populations. Outside of the northeast, brook trout can now be found all the way west to California, northwest to Washington and southwest to Arizona, as well as in many states in between. Anglers may still pursue big, native fish in the Canadian waters of Manitoba, Ontario, Quebec, and Labrador...

Brook trout evolved on the salmonid tree as a member of the char sub-group. They have proven their ability to survive in cold, harsh environments, conditions in which members of the true trout family could not comfortably reside year-round. The brook trout thrive in such waters and, accompanied by the artic char, are cold-water champions. Contrary to their name, brook trout are found in lakes and streams, as long as the water is cold and well-oxygenated; optimum water temperatures are around 55 degrees Fahrenheit. Some brook trout which inhabit coastal rivers also spend time in the saltwater. These fish are commonly called "coasters" or "salters."

The coloring of the brook trout is olive-green to dark brown on the back, with lightening on the sides, to eventual silvery white along the belly. The fins are laced in white. The brookie, sometimes called a "speckled trout," also has colorful spotting along its sides. During the spawning period, as normal coloring intensifies, the brook trout may be the world's most beautiful fresh-

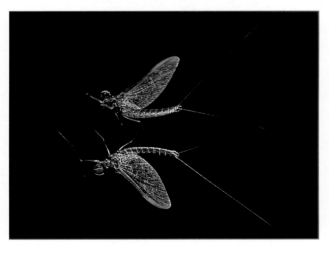

water fish. Especially upon the males, the belly develops an orange-red color, and spotting becomes brilliantly hued with halos, including colors of blue, purple, and yellow. When breeding, the males may develop a hook at the front of their lower jaw.

Brook trout typically spawn in the fall, preferring sand and gravel areas. During this time, there are often large aggregations of fish either along a lake shoreline or at the headwaters of a stream. Females dig the redd, and within a day deposit their eggs; depending on her size, the female will lay between 100 and 5,000 eggs. The female then usually resides close to the redd. The males will dart in and fertilize the eggs. Hatching will vary depending on the region and habitat, but usually eggs will hatch 50 to 100 days after fertilization. As the brook trout grow, they prove a carnivorous and voracious fish, eating all types of insects, crustaceans and other fish, including cannibalizing their own.

The Minipi River system in Labrador is a brook trout fishery worth special recognition. There is prolific aquatic life in the form of caddis and mayflies that prompt the big fish in its waters, fish which weigh frequently in excess of five pounds, to look towards the surface for their nourishment. In this watershed, the fish have been protected and nurtured throughout the past several decades by thoughtful management initiated by Lee Wulff and extending to the Cooper family, who currently operates the fishing lodges on the drainage. There are fly fishermen who have fished the Minipi annually for the past 20-plus years and have kept meticulous records on the fish caught and released. They comment on how the fishing today exceeds the fishery of old, both in size and number of fish; this is obviously a unique situation in today's world of shrinking natural environments and is a tribute to the strong conservation principles practiced.

Casting to sipping cruisers during the long hours of dusk in the far north of Labrador.

Hiking up a small tributary in search of giant brookies

Evening drake hatch on the Minipi

Think it will rain?

A shoreside barbecue of small brookies

THE PERMIT

The big, black tail popped up in about three feet of water. We could see the body attached to that tail so we knew we were looking at a big permit, probably over twenty-five pounds. We were poling down a ridge between two flats. A few inches of crystal-clear tidal flow rolled gently over the ridge that separated us from the tail on the other side...

It was an isolated area that was not easily accessed from either the mainland or an island-based lodge. We'd been fishing the vicinity for three days using a mothership as our base of operations and hadn't encountered another angler.

Nothing can more rapidly raise the pulse rate of a saltwater fly fisherman than a large, single permit feeding aggressively. This fish met all the criteria. Sweat started to bead on the angler's forehead as the guide positioned the skiff for a cast. One last time, the caster checked to see that he wasn't standing on the 60 feet of fly line coiled at his feet on the casting platform. The line was perfect, away from his feet and tangle free.

Martin suggested, "Now, put it five feet in front of him." The angler made a few false casts then released the crab pattern. As the fly headed toward its intended target, the permit made a sharp turn and swam directly away from the skiff. The fly landed about ten feet short of the fish's tail. It was still feeding, just in a slightly different spot.

Again, Martin repositioned the skiff; again the caster made ready; and again the fly set sail toward the nose of the permit. Again, the fish turned and moved off while the fly was in the air. His tail broke the surface as he feasted on some tasty morsel fifteen feet beyond where the crab pattern settled into the clear water.

The boat was getting close to the shallow ridge and the risk of the skiff's bottom scraping coral and scaring off the quarry was high. The angler stepped out of the skiff to continue his stalk on foot, stepping cautiously, hoping not to noisily crunch any coral.

Still easily visible, the permit had moved about 20 feet further up the ridge. The fisherman moved tentatively, needing a few more steps to get within range. The palpable tension in the warm tropical air emanated from the determined demeanor of the caster.

Again the fish's head went down to feed and his big, black sickle tail was waving above the surface. Again, the caster let his cast go, but this time the fish did not move – until the fly hit the water. Though he did not appear to be spooked, he did swim off the shallow ledge of the flat and disappeared. With his shoulders slumped in disappointment, the angler looked back at the guide. Martin motioned for the caster to stay still. If the fish were to reappear, he didn't want any sudden movements to permanently drive him away.

Hoping for one more attempt, both angler and guide scanned the water up and down the ridge for the next five minutes. It was McCord, from his more elevated perch on the skiff, who saw the reappearance of that big tail. The fish had migrated about 100 feet up the ridge and was actively feeding again. McCord pointed and the angler soon picked up the rippling motion on the smooth waters.

Quickly, but carefully, the caster moved up the ridge toward the fish. After more than 20 minutes of stalking this fish, it appeared that he might get another chance. He slowed as he approached casting distance; the permit continued to show himself, chasing his dinner. A false cast and then the fly was away, zinging toward the target – but it landed short. As the fisherman began to pick up the fly to recast, McCord whispered, "don't move it – he's coming." Sure enough, the fish had seen the fly and was beginning to vibrate with anticipation as he moved toward it. Everything looked perfect – with an edge of excitement in his voice, McCord said, "heeeee's cooooomin."

Just as the permit arrived at the fly, there was an explosion in the water. Both guide and fisherman thought the permit had eaten the feathery crab. But, as the fish got close enough to inhale the fly, he had apparently seen something he didn't like and was gone......this time forever, at least for this day.

Ahhhhhh, permit fishing. It takes a high level of tolerance for frustration. And that's what makes it so special.

FLY FISHING'S HOLY GRAIL

As revered as the permit is as a shallow water gamefish, it's surprising there is so little information available about them. We know they can live in deep water and that they frequent the flats in search of crabs and other crustaceans (much the same as a bonefish). Permit exist from the coastal waters of the mid-Atlantic states south to Brazil. The greatest concentrations are found in south Florida, Belize and the Sian Ka'an Biosphere (Ascension Bay and vicinity) of the Mexican Yucatan.

...Even the issue of the permit's spawning season is not documented. Two renowned saltwater fly anglers, Jeffrey Cardenas and Winston Moore, responded in similar fashion to the question about the spawning season...

Cardenas: "Permit are still a mystery to me and I've spent nearly 25 years fishing hard for them. Whenever I have one 'sharked,' I rush to recover the carcass and I have found roe in them in both late March and late October." Moore: "My best guess is they spawn in Belize the last half of April through May. However, if you talk to ten different Belizean guides you'll get ten different theories."

The Atlantic Permit is a member of the pompano family and has a number of relatives. There is a Pacific Permit in the family, but even less is known about him, as he is not pursued with the fervor of his Atlantic cousin. When the permit is small, its appearance can cause it to be confused with the other pompanos, but there is not another relative that attains his size. Winston Moore has taken one in Ascension Bay (photo below) estimated in the 50 pound range, and several over 40 pounds have been documented. Even a five-pound permit is reason for celebration, especially if it's an angler's first permit on a fly.

Why are permit so challenging to catch on shallow flats with a fly? The answer starts with their nervous demeanor as they move from deep channels onto "skinny water" flats. On the flat, they become an easy target for a variety of sea birds, sharks and barracuda. This vulnerability makes them very sensitive to any sound or sight that is out of the ordinary. Its huge, specialized eyes provide the permit with tremendous vision to determine what is edible. And, they usually swim in an erratic fashion, making it difficult to determine where to place the fly. Often, a cast to a cruising fish that looks like it will be perfect at the outset ends up being ten yards from the fish as the permit has changed directions while the fly was in the air.

There are two situations that give the angler the best opportunity to get an "eat" from a permit. The first is a school of three to ten fish slowly cruising together. In this situation, sometimes the competitive instincts will overcome their normal cautious approach. The second opportunity occurs when a permit is agressively tailing with its nose buried in the bottom chasing some delectable morsel. Often a fish in this focused feeding mode will allow the angler to get very close and will respond impulsively to a well placed fly.

It could be argued that the most exciting sight in the arena of saltwater fly fishing is a big, black permit tail waving above a shallow water flat. However, there is no argument that releasing a fly-caught permit taken on the flats is the "holy grail" of fly fishing.

Measurements put this Ascension Bay permit, taken by permit guru Winston Moore, at about fifty pounds. It may have been a world record, but was never officially weighed before released.

Who forgot the net?!

Found! School of small, tailing permit…

The Cast…

The Strip…

The TAKE!

The Fish!

This coastline connects two of the worlds great permit fisheries: Ascension Bay and Espiritu Santo Bay on the Mexican Yucatan and, at the top of the photo, Belize.

THE
RAINBOW
TROUT

The three of us huddled at the head of the pool. The dense, temperate rainfor-est pressed in all around. Brilliant green foliage sprinkled with bright flowers of unknown names hemmed in the riverbanks. A thin layer of mist clung to the cool surface as the shallow, crystalline water flowed over polished, rounded river stones…

...It was a pristine watershed, an unnamed stream; one of many which drain the mountains surrounding the fjords of Chilean Patagonia. Fueling our anticipation, its population of big rainbows had very rarely seen an artificial fly...

Our predicament was obvious. The river flowed in at the top of the pool in a gentle riffle, and exited about 100 feet down in the same manner. The small river, perhaps better described as a large stream, was 40 feet across at the widest point. A logjam was haphazardly piled against the far bank about halfway down the pool. Gently finning parallel to the logjam were two rainbows, easily in the 7-pound plus range; they were lined up nose-to-tail in about three feet of water. The fish were maybe 12 inches out from the tangle of wood that would surely and quickly claim any fly or leader that strayed into it. The trout looked strong as they idly held their spots, patiently waiting for their next meal.

Our guide, Frederico, had initially spotted the fish as the three of us walked upstream. The stalk then began. The over-hanging jungle would not allow an upstream cast from the tail of the pool. Frederico, my wife Michelle (a fly fishing novice) and I slowly and carefully skirted the edge of the stream, keeping a low profile as we virtually crawled around the perimeter of the pool. It was difficult to resist throwing a cast as we made our way, but we had agreed that the ideal beginner's cast was from the top of the run. The bright red stripes adorning the sides of the fish were visible from seemingly every angle.

We achieved the head of the pool without spooking our quarry. Michelle prepared to cast. It was a challenging presentation, and she had to remain on her knees to keep a low profile. The cast went about 30 feet at a downstream angle, and Michelle promptly followed with a few line mends. We could see the bead-headed wooly bugger flut-

tering and flashing as it drifted into the pool. It appeared to be perfectly in line with the fish.

Upon Frederico's word, Michelle tightened up on the line and slowly began to strip in line as the fly swung toward the logs. The fly cleared the tip of the logjam by mere inches. The lead fish responded, moving forward and up into the current. A wake formed behind the fly and developed into the broad back of a big, hungry rainbow trout. A furious explosion sent water spraying everywhere. Michelle's rod bent deep as she reared back against the weight of what was obviously a heavy fish.

I gave an excited holler as Frederico, his Chilean accented English full of adrenaline, began offering advice to Michelle. This was a big fish. What would it do? The pool was only about a 100 feet long; I thought for sure it would rocket downriver toward the fjord.

The fish opted to stay on the bottom, angrily moving up and down the length of the pool, seemingly undecided in its movements. Michelle kept the pressure on, attempting to prevent the fish from bolting the hole and steering it clear of the logjam.

The movements of the fish were easy to follow in the shallow, clear water. It repeatedly flashed its brilliant colors and shook its head in an attempt to rid itself of the fly. Thankfully Frederico had tied on heavy leader material; this fish tested every pound of its rating strength.

After what seemed an eternity of battling, the fish began to tire from the relentless pressure. It gave a sideways roll, showing us its vibrant red stripe and greenish back, then dove and hunkered down at the bottom of the deepest part of the pool. Due to the size of the fish and its holding pattern in the current, Michelle could not retrieve any further line by reeling. With no other alternative, she clamped down on the line and began slowly backing up the bank, pulling the trout towards shore. It proved an effective measure.

Frederico tailed it, and everyone shouted in victory. It was indeed a tremendous catch; we all huddled around the fish as it was revived. We guessed the weight around eight pounds, much bigger than any rainbow I had ever released. Even Frederico was impressed. One of Michelle's first fish on a fly was indeed a memorable catch. (*Photos on opposite page*)

Whether it is a native fish refusing

a seemingly flawless presentation

of a Pale Morning Dun EVERYMAN'S FISH

or a hatchery-raised fish

engulfing a wad of power-

bait in the local fishing

pond, the rainbow trout is

everyman's fish. Coupled

with its reputation as fine

table-fare, the rainbow's resourceful

ability to reside in diverse watersheds

makes it perhaps the most acces-

sible and pursued fish in the world

today...

...Indeed its range is far-reaching, from the islands of New Zealand to the northern waters of Alaska, and from the mountains of New Mexico to Eastern Europe...

The rainbow possesses the various qualities required to place it in the elite of gamefish. They can be an intelligent and sensitive quarry, especially for the fly fisherman. You may repeatedly consult your fly box trying to find the correct imitation, only to eventually put the fish down with nary a rise. To rid itself of the hook, a 'bow will often leap repeatedly into the air, providing a spectacular display of determination. They also have the endurance to make long, sustained runs followed by a slugfest before conceding. Particularly river-born fish have an inner strength developed throughout their lives from holding in currents that provides an additional advantage when trying to escape the net. The rainbow trout can grow quite large; the current fly-caught record is over thirty pounds. Combine all of these factors with the inherent spotted, rainbow-hued beauty of this specimen and it is understandable why it is considered such a prized fish.

Contrary to other trout species – brown trout, for example – the 'bow is definitely a fast-water, current-loving trout, seeking out highly oxygenated waters. Rainbows, while being a delicate fish, can tolerate a wide range of water temperatures, from the low 30s Fahrenheit up to the mid 70s. The rainbow can live past ten years of age;

the subspecies from Eagle Lake, California is one of the longest living strains, reportedly achieving ages of over 11 years. There are numerous rainbow trout subspecies, having names such as Kamloops, Kern River, McKenzie River, Eagle Lake, and McCloud River rainbows, to name a few. Rainbows can also breed with other members of the trout family, such as cutthroat and golden trout, at times creating unusually brilliant hybrids. The life cycle of the wild rainbow trout begins in a female-dug redd, usually in a tail-out or riffle of a stream. The spawning act lasts mere seconds, as the male and female deposit eggs and milt simultaneously into the redd, followed by the female finning loose gravel over the area. The spawning season is typically in the spring; indeed, this spawning cycle, depending on your regional location, often defines the fishing season for many fly fishermen.

The adaptive abilities of the rainbow trout are further exemplified by its ocean-going brethren, known as steelhead. Explaining the steelhead's anadromous behavior – meaning migrating up rivers from the sea to breed in fresh water – can be a complex task. The instinct arguably evolved during early geological times as the fish adapted to periods of glaciation and subsequent tributary availability. Whatever the origins of motivation, this tough, hard-nosed fish has been documented to travel thousands of miles to return to its original freshwater birthplace to start a new life cycle. Steelhead are predominately silver, although they frequently develop the stream rainbow's signature red band as more time is spent in freshwater. The passion and zeal with which steelhead are pursued by dedicated enthusiasts is rarely matched in the fishing world. Whether in freshwater or salt, the rainbow trout is worthy of its fame and notoriety.

The life cycle of the Alaskan salmon, from the egg to the spent adult, provides the nutrients for a rich aquatic habitat that supports a great variety of wildlife ranging from large grizzlies to giant rainbows.

ALASKA

- WARNING
Absolutely NO
AEROSOL BEAR
REPELLENT Devices
Allowed on
Peninsula Airways
Passenger Aircraft

THE HUNTER
BECOMES THE HUNTED

The Hues of the
RAINBOW

British Columbia flyout on the Blackwater.

Stalking sippers on the North Platte.

TROPICAL
EVENINGS

It was nearly dark as we shut the motor down and drifted slowly to our destination. Stars were twinkling brightly in the off-shore, unpolluted, and cloudless Belizean sky as the final remnants of a spectacular sunset were fading on the western horizon. We'd planned to be here a little earlier to try to duplicate the exciting surface activity we'd experienced the night before, but were detained by a school of tailing bonefish with the setting sun glinting off their fins and

...The previous evening, this mangrove channel, an area not unlike many mangrove channels off the Belize coast, had provided an hour of great thrills...

Behind us was a large bay, where as the tide pulled out, it funneled like a river through this small 50-foot wide gap in the mangroves. About 15 minutes before total darkness settled in, the activity had started. First it was just an occasional "pop" as a horse-eye jack ate something the current was delivering to him. In the dim light, we couldn't make out the feeding fish, but we could hear them. Whatever they were eating was on or very near the surface, and their feeding activity created a distinctive sound.

It had been a balmy tropical evening to remember – warm air and gentle sea breezes with a brilliant star-studded sky. But it was the fishing excitement that had made the experience so memorable. For about 45 minutes, we'd enjoyed frantic activity in the dark by casting our black foam poppers to the resonance of a feeding frenzy. Several feisty four- to six-pound horse-eye jacks were released. Occasionally, there was a loud splash that our guide explained was a tarpon among the jacks. We verified the tarpon explanation by hooking up with one of them and being doused with spray as he lifted his big body out of the water and came crashing down a few feet from the boat. We were disappointed when the tarpon threw the hook on his second jump, but large snappers joining the fray helped keep us focused on the next cast. As fast as the action had started, it abruptly stopped. Whatever had triggered the gathering in this particular area was over, and the water and evening grew quiet.

Hoping for a repeat performance of the night before, my daughter, Holli, and I began stripping out our lines. The tide was flowing strong and we were anchored in exactly the same spot as the previous evening. Everything appeared the same except for the silence. The aggressive feeding and accompanying sounds were missing. I flashed back to the many times I had tried to replicate an angling situation, hoping for the same results that had occurred another time in the same place. Never happened. The great moments in fly fishing seemed to be singular events, never to be relived.

As I was considering that maybe we were wasting our time and that dinner sounded like a good idea, Holli asked, "Did you hear that?" It was a tiny reminder of the excitement of yesterday – only one feeding fish. It fed again, and then again. Lacking the crescendo of the night before, something was eating and moving a lot of water about 40 or 50 feet below where we were stationed. In the light of my headlamp, I saw Holli look at me and I gave her the nod that said, "OK, go ahead and take the cast – I'll watch."

The black popper whistled down the channel and the noisy retrieve began, pushing water as it came upstream against the flow. Zilch. She repeated the cast several times with the same result. Nothing. However, we could still hear the fish feeding and swirling in the current. Maybe we weren't reaching the fish?

Casting a fly line after dark has its own set of liabilities. Many things can go wrong in the pitch black. Instead of lengthening her cast, she asked the guide to release another ten feet of the anchor line to move us closer to the sound.

The first cast after the repositioning of the skiff proved the effort worthwhile. There was a grab. Holli leaned into the hook-set. We soon realized this wasn't another horse-eye jack. We could hear the fish break the surface, and when he crashed back down, the phosphorous-enhanced spray was visible, even from our distance. It was a tarpon and it didn't appear to be a small, mangrove "baby tarpon." In a few seconds the fish was airborne again, and this time when he returned to earth, we could hear the breaking of mangrove branches. He'd thrown himself into the thick growth bordering the channel. The thrashing in the brush continued for what seemed like minutes, but was probably only seconds.

Holding our breath, we waited to see what would happen next. We couldn't see a thing, and we didn't know if he was hung up in the mangroves. The chances of the leader being caught up and tangled in the bushes seemed high. After a few tense, helpless seconds, line began peeling off the reel as the fish screamed down the channel.

The ensuing tug of war between angler and tarpon was one that has been repeated thousands of times. After some 30 minutes, Holli had the fish close enough that we could see his silver scales reflecting our light. What a sight! It wasn't a giant, but appeared to be in the 40-pound range.

After a few more minutes our guide had the fish under control. A flash photo was snapped and the fish carefully released. "Sight fishing" this wasn't – but "sound fishing" can be just as exhilarating. (*Photo on opposite page*)

WHEN THE SUN GOES DOWN IN THE TROPICS...

....the waters come alive. Stalking tailing permit or bonefish as the evening sun glints off their fins is a memorable experience. After the sun dips below the horizon and daytime inches toward the night, the flats' possibilities fade with the falling light. At this same time, a door opens to an entirely different arena of fly fishing opportunities...

...Since 1986, we have been fortunate to experience many spectacular tropical sunsets while fly fishing the low light and the following initial period of darkness. The entire food chain, starting with the smallest micro-organisms, become active as the sunlight fades...

With the approach of darkness, many species of saltwater game fish become increasingly active and aggressive.

Using a mothership as our base of operations while fly fishing Belize' coastal flats and interspersed channels has been the key that has opened this tropical evening door. Rather than being locked into a "drinks and dinner schedule" at a land-based lodge during this productive hour, the mothership allows us to be on the water throughout the final stages of fading daylight. Meals are prepared around our fishing schedule rather than us adjusting the timing of our fishing to a structured mealtime.

In the mangrove roots, the fall of darkness brings an increased boldness as snook and baby tarpon become more likely to leave their sanctuary to venture into the surrounding shallows.

A thrilling aspect of fishing tropical evenings comes from some eight to fifteen foot deep channels adjoining shallower flats and mangrove islands. Except in instances where fish are found feeding near the surface and can be taken with poppers, this fishing is primarily sink-tip, streamer-type fishing. Snappers, jacks, permit and especially large tarpon can destroy the peacefulness of an eighty-degree evening.

The most productive evening channel fishing takes place during the 30 minutes prior to dark, and the first 15 minutes after the final curtain of darkness has dropped. It's a very narrow window of opportunity. Usually, even when the bite is very aggressive, the action drops off sharply shortly after the last rays of the sun disappear from the horizon.

Seeing an 80 to 100+ pound tarpon silhouetted against the setting sun as it leaps six feet clear of the water is one of those fly fishing sights that is never forgotten. It's also a thrill to hear a large tarpon crashing to the surface after repeated jumps when darkness prevents you from seeing anything but a faint glimpse of white spray.

Being on the water with a fly rod in hand during warm Belizean evenings can become a treasured fly fishing adventure.

REASONS FOR A
LATE DINNER...

MORE REASONS...

THE LATE DINNER

EVOLUTION OF A FLY FISHERMAN

For a passionate fly fishing father, there are not many thrills in life that top watching your son or daughter develop as a fly fisher. First, you notice their enthusiasm for the outdoors and the environment that makes fly fishing special. They begin to find a way to go fishing without your involvement. Outside of your influence, they develop their own fly fishing circle of friends. It's then you know that the passion is present and it's growing. Next, comes the reality that they have developed abilities that outstrip what you have taught them about the sport. They're throwing a longer line or they're back casting the entire fly line when the extent of your back casting talent is about 50 feet. You watch them work a feeding fish with skills you don't have. It's all great stuff and you begin to realize you have someone with whom you can share a lifetime of fly fishing thrills.

"Look what I did, Mom"
– Scott brings home dinner.

Catfish Slayer

Graduates to saltwater flats fly fishing – first permit (taken before Dad got his first on a fly – think the Gumby shirt was the key)

It's In The Eyes:
A Look That Could Worry A Mother

It's a long stretch, both geographically and fly fishing environment-wise, from a 8.25 pound Labrador Brook Trout to a 40 pound Belize tarpon, but the angler's look is the same. Is something wrong with that boy or can it just be the fish?

A Cover Boy

RODS, REELS AND CAMERAS...
Fishing With My Dad

The Hunt began on the waters of the Fall River in Northern California about 23 years ago. To that point, my dad had wielded a fly rod in Alaska a time or two, but he wasn't a big threat to the fish. I just loved to fish period, and at the age of 12 was all about minnows and bobbers still.

But as with everything in his life, when dad decided to do something, he did it at 110%. So he found what was deemed the best fly fishery in the state, located the best guide (thank you, John Ogden, for all the lessons) and off we went. The experience took hold of us with a feverish pitch, and we wanted more.

As I rode around on my father's substantial coattails, we began traveling the world. I was a lucky kid indeed. Dad would research the best international locations for the type of fish I had only read about. Over the years, through our varied experiences, we both became good fly fisher-men. Eventually dad began capturing our adventures on film, and over time has developed into one of the leading flyfishing photographers in the world. As his fishing partner, his passion for photography certainly had a big upside, as I found myself perched in the bow of the boat far more than 50% of the time as he began to focus on capturing the experience on film. Then came the new "dress code" – brightly colored collared shirt, some goofy looking hat, and for gracious sake, do not forget the bandana (as long as it matches the shorts). I resisted for awhile, but eventually fell in line.

So here we are today. Dad has retired from his primary business, only to start another. He now books trips to all the best flyfishing destinations worldwide. And he has been to most all of them. And then there is *The Hunt*. Although this book has been a family production, it was certainly my father's dogged persistence that made it happen. And it happened at 110%.

Book is done – let's go fishing, Dad. And maybe set that camera down for awhile.

GUIDES & OUTFITTERS

The Hunt would not have been possible without the many outstanding guides and outfitters we have fished with throughout the years. In addition to leading the way to the fish, many of these individuals actually clicked the shutter on some of the photos in the book.

Abarca, Fernando - Puyuhuapi, Chile
Allen, Lonnie - Three Rivers Ranch, Eastern Idaho
Allen, Mitch - Three Rivers Ranch, Eastern Idaho
Aspinall, Craig - Poronui Ranch, New Zealand
Ayuso, Pedro - Belize
Baker, Duane - Florida Keys
Barr, Emmet - Florida Keys
Best, Ray - Minipi River, Labrador
Birt, Nigel - South Island, New Zealand
Blackwell, John - Moose Lake Lodge/Dean River, BC
Bryngelson, Rex - La Posada de los Farios, Chile
Burke, Andy - Northern California
Caamal, Pedro - Boca Paila/Casa Blanca, Ascension Bay
Chapman, Mike - French Polynesia
Cole, Ian - South Island, New Zealand
Cooper, Jack - Minipi River, Labrador
Cooper, Lorraine - Minipi River, Labrador
Costello, Mike - Pacific Adventures, Northern California
Dawes, Mike - World Cast Outfitters, Eastern Idaho
Dickinson, John - Florida Keys
Dzul, Victor - Boca Paila, Sian Kaan, Mexico
Escudero, David - Casa Blanca, Ascension Bay, Mexico
Fox, Jeff - Southern Oregon
Gomez, Edwardo - Boca Paila, Sian Kaan, Mexico
Guptill, Howard - Minipi River, Labrador
Hall, Kyle - North Platte Lodge, Wyoming
Halson, Ed - Blanket Bay, New Zealand
Hamill, John - North Island, New Zealand
Hansen, Russell - Bruners Lodge, New Zealand
Happersett, Bill - Jackson Hole, Wyoming
Hartman, Grant - Baja Anglers, Mexico
Henry, Alex - French Polynesia
Heywood, Scott - Kamchatka, Russia
Hyde, Brent - Lake Rotoroa Lodge, South Island
Jansen, Frans - Isla Monita, Chile
King, John - Lake Rotoroa Lodge, New Zealand
Klingler, Royce - Three Rivers Ranch, Eastern Idaho
Lavallee, Willie - Minipi River, Labrador
Lovell, Doug - Fish First, Northern California
Lyon, Matt - Henry's Fork Lodge, Eastern Idaho
McCord, Martin - The Meca, Belize
McKenzie, Jack - North Island, New Zealand

McKinley, Mark - Minipi River, Labrador
Mullen, Skip - Three Rivers Ranch, Eastern Idaho
Myers, Dean - The Meca, Belize
Negri, Pablo - Chile
Neymour, Ivan - Tranquility Hill, Andros Island
Oas, Dan - World Cast Outfitters, Eastern Idaho
Ogden, John - Fall River, Northern California
Payne, Kevin - South Island, New Zealand
Pike, David - Lake Rotoroa Lodge, New Zealand
Rainey, Jim - North Island, New Zealand
Reid, Clark - Poronui Ranch, New Zealand
Reilly, Eve - Poronui Ranch, New Zealand
Rowland, Tom - Florida Keys and Jackson Hole, Wyoming
Saelzer, Rodrigo - Puyuhuapi, Chile
Sandoval, Rodrigo - Chile
Schuerger, Greg - Sweeney's Sports, Northern California
Settles, Bobby - Casa Blanca/Playa Blanca, Ascension Bay
Shortland, Jason - South Island, New Zealand
Silverman, Joel - Paloma Lodge, Chile
Smith, Allan - Crocodile Bay, Costa Rica
Snow, Chad - Minipi River, Labrador
Taylor, Brent - Paloma Lodge, Chile
Taylor, Liam - South Island, New Zealand
Tuuta, Greg - North Island, New Zealand
Valentine, Eric - Qamea, Fiji
Van de Loo, Paul - South Island, New Zealand
Ward, Dennis - North Island, New Zealand
Ward, Monte - Katmai Lodge, Alaska
Westby, Avi - The Seaduction, Belize
Westby, Carlton - The Meca, Belize
Westby, Charles - The Seaduction, Belize
White, Fletcher - World Cast Outfitters, Eastern Idaho
Young, Carol - The Meca, Belize
Young, Junior - Belize
Yrazabal, Chris - Los Roques/French Polynesia
Zoll, Nick - Casa Blanca, Ascension Bay, Mexico

PHOTOGRAPHIC LOCATIONS

Page Number And Location Of Photo

Inside Front Cover: Tarpon scales
1   Minipi River, Labrador
2, 3   Eastern Idaho
4, 5   Tarpon flat, Belize
6   Minipi River
7   Bonefish flat, Belize
8, 9   South Island, NZ
10   Chilean Fjords
10, 11   South Island, NZ
11   Chilean Fjords
12, 13   Bonefish flat, Belize
14   Teton River, Eastern Idaho
14, 15   Henry's Fork, Eastern Idaho
15   Belize sunset
15   Chilean Brown
16, 17   Chilean Andes
18, 19   Bonefish flat, Ascension Bay
20, 21   South Island, NZ
22   Tarpon flat, Belize
24   Henry's Fork, Eastern Idaho
26   Tailing Permit, Ascension Bay
28   Eastern Idaho
30, 31   Belize
32   Belize
33   Florida Keys
34, 35   Belize
36   Florida Keys
37   Belize
38, 39   Florida Keys
40   Florida Keys
41   Lighthouse Reef, Belize
42, 43   Belize
44t.   Belize
44b.   Ascension Bay
46, 47   North Island, NZ
48   South Island, NZ
50, 51   South Island, NZ
52   Chilean Andes
53   South Island, NZ
56, 57   South Island, NZ
58   Chilean Andes
60, 61   South Island, NZ
62, 63   South Pacific
64   Belize
66, 67   Belize
68   Florida Keys
69   Andros Island, Bahamas
72, 73   Ascension Bay
76   Belize
77   Ascension Bay (RS)
78, 79   Teton River, Eastern Idaho
82, 83   Teton River, Eastern Idaho
84   Eastern Idaho
85   South Fork of the Snake, Idaho
88   South Fork of the Snake, Idaho

90, 91   Eastern Idaho
92, 93   Belize
94   Ascension Bay
95   South Pacific
97   Belize
100   Ascension Bay
101t.   Crocodile Bay, Costa Rica
102, 103   Belize
105   Ascension Bay
106 – 119 Minipi River, Labrador
120, 121   Belize
122   Ascension Bay
124, 125   Nicaragua
126   Ascension Bay
127   Ascension Bay
128, 129   Belize
130   Belize
131   Belize
132   Belize
134, 135   South Island, NZ
136   Chilean Fjords
137   Putah Creek, No. California
138, 139   Henry's Fork, Eastern Idaho
140   North Island, NZ
141   North Island, NZ
142   Chilean Andes
143   North Island, NZ
148, 149   North Island, NZ
150 – 161 Belize
166t.   Minipi River, Labrador
166b.   Florida Keys
Inside Rear Cover: Brook trout flank
Back cover: South Island, New Zealand